DEEP
RED

∽∽∽∽

University of Central Florida • *Contemporary Poetry Series*

DEEP
RED

∽∽∽∽∽

Poems by
Rawdon Tomlinson

University Press of Florida
Gainesville / Tallahassee / Tampa / Boca Raton
Pensacola / Orlando / Miami / Jacksonville

00 99 98 97 96 95 6 5 4 3 2 1

Library of Congress Cataloging-in-Publication Data

Tomlinson, Rawdon, 1947–

Deep red: poems / by Rawdon Tomlinson.

p. cm. — (University of Central Florida contemporary poetry series)

Includes bibliographical references (p.).

ISBN 0-8130-1346-1 (acid-free paper)

I. Title. II. Series: Contemporary poetry series (Orlando, Fla.)

PS3570.048D4   1994

811'.54—dc20   94-40998

The University Press of Florida is the scholarly publishing agency for the State University System of Florida, comprised of Florida A & M University, Florida Atlantic University, Florida International University, Florida State University, University of Central Florida, University of Florida, University of North Florida, University of South Florida, and University of West Florida.

University Press of Florida

15 Northwest 15th Street

Gainesville, FL 32611

*For My Mother and Father
and My Grandparents,
and for Karen, Caitlin, Eryn,
Rawdon and Claire*

CONTENTS

ACKNOWLEDGMENTS

Some of the poems in this volume first appeared in the following journals:

Abraxas: "Raggedy Ann"
Alabama Literary Review: "Mother Waiting"
Atlanta Review: "Splitting Wood"
Birmingham Poetry Review: "Daybreak on the North Fork" and "Great Horned Owl"
The Chattahoochee Review: "Moonman"
College English: "Ballad of a Road Boy"
Commonweal: "Mr. Norwood"
Cottonwood: "Alta"
Cumberland Poetry Review: "Original Sin and Forgiveness at Restland"
Dalhousie Review (Canada): "Deep Red"
The Dekalb Literary Arts Journal: "Easter 1954"
Fiddlehead (Canada): "Miscarriage"
Galley Sail Review: "Whiteout"
Hiram Poetry Review: "Birth," "Closing Time at the Zoo," "Fat People at the Amusement Park" and "A Good Night's Sleep"
Hollins Critic: "Signs" and "Run-Off"
Interim: "Mother's Roses" and "Winter Wheat"
Kansas Quarterly: "Elk at Dusk" and "For James Riley"
Laurel Review: "Night Wind"
Minnesota Review: "Lightning-Struck Boy"
New Mexico Humanities Review: "Trains" and "Pine and Aspen"
Northeast: "Cunningham Burns, Electrician"
Poet and Critic: "Pain Fugue," "Letter in Middle Age to My Ex-Wife, Not Mailed," and "Coyote Nights"
Poet Lore: "How They Live"

Quarry (Canada): "The Cabin at Elk Falls" and "Lightning-Struck Pine"

Quarry West: "Christmas 1953"

River City (formerly *Memphis State Review*): "Creede, 1931" and "Under the Hackberry"

San Jose Studies: "Sangre de Cristo, July 4"

Sewanee Review: "Visions of a Bone Hunter"

South Carolina Review: "Father's Disaster Tale"

South Dakota Review: "Evil and Flower" and "With Caitlin after Rain"

South Florida Poetry Journal: "Red Ants"

Tar River Poetry: "Teenage Funeral"

The Texas Review: "This Morning You Will Wake"

University of Windsor Review (Canada): "Crawdads"

Visions International: "Indiahoma"

Weber Studies: "Of an Evening"

Wisconsin Review: "The Sunday School Teacher"

Writers' Forum: "Ancestors," "How the Dead Come Back," "Lost" and "Breakdown"

Certain of these poems also appeared in the following anthologies:

Full Circle (Charlotte Poetry Project): "Moonman" and "Evil and Flower"

The Tyranny of the Normal (Kent State University Press): "Fat People at the Amusement Park"

Spreading the Word: Editors on Poetry (The Bench Press): "Fat People at the Amusement Park"

Wingbone: Poetry from Colorado (Sudden Jungle Press): "Ancestors" and "Deep Red"

I am especially grateful to Victoria McCabe, Karen Swenson, and Karen Tomlinson for their comments and suggestions on the poems and their steady support.

I also wish to thank Gwen Ashbaugh for instructing me in the mysteries of the Macintosh Classic.

The epigraph to "The Cabin at Elk Falls" is from "Poem on His Birthday," *The Collected Poems of Dylan Thomas,* and is reprinted by permission of New Directions Publishing Corporation. The epigraph to "Lightning-Struck Pine" is from "Evening in the Sanitarium," by Louise Bogan, from *The Blue Estuaries: Poems 1923–1968,* and is reprinted by permission of The Ecco Press, 1977. The epigraph to "How the Dead Come Back" is from "Watching the Horror Movie," by Walter Hall, from *Miners Getting Off the Graveyard,* and is reprinted by permission of Burning Deck. The epigraph to "For James Riley" is from *Deaths Duell,* by John Donne, and is reprinted by permission of David R. Godine, 1973.

I
DEEP RED

∾∾∾∾

ANCESTORS

They stand in front of the big fenders
And headlights, bulbous chrome grille
With Indian chief hood ornament
Which lights up in the dark.

In the background is a magnolia tree
And part of a house, a clothesline strung
Across gray space; a black and white
Bulldog sits at their feet

Making its smudged face of teeth.
Each thing is in its place:
Nothing worried about their eyes,
No problem with belief.

They're confident about the truth,
Sporting short fat ties
With gold watch chains hanging from vests
Of white, baggy suits—

Yet nothing says they're aloof or braggart.
Things are in their places:
The dime cigars they hold spoofing; spats
Shined—parts known by heart.

The women are inside the house
Finishing the chicken;
The thin one married to the son
Still dreams of being a nurse,

And doesn't talk much to the other
Who married again for fun.
At church they sang and took communion
This bright, airy Easter,

And now they'll go for a ride in the country,
And eat chicken under
Some big oak at the edge of a pasture,
And everything will be

"Pretty as a picture," set
With only a cloud or two
Drifting across a spotless sky,
Everyone forgets . . .

The lean years behind; the children
Growing up strong, knowing
Right from wrong; and business booming—
A time sweet as Eden:

The fields of wheat like a table run
Smooth and green to the horizon;
And the cows graze painted
Into the blue air and sun.

The Kodak clicks, and they sigh out
Breath, joking, ready
To go, as the women emerge from the dark
Screen door in big hats,

With picnic basket, mocking a gesture
Of impatience; the engine starts,
Dresses are smoothed and doors shut—
No one knows who took the picture.

UNDER THE HACKBERRY

The afternoon is sparrows and light.

I watch the dizzy ants, waiting for one
to slip into the grain smooth cone
of an ant lion invisible at bottom,
pincers cocked.

Grandmother comes and goes
through the dark screen door
carrying baskets of white.

Clothespinned above
the bed of irises,
sheets breathe in and out like sails
in the doldrums,

as though a story was being told
which embraced everything
and everyone,
held in the day's dream
of green slowly nodding.

Grandmother continues living her other,
parallel life, loneliness
buried with her husband,

while I play in the dirt,
his namesake,
unaccompanied today
by the floating night fears,

as though each of us had journeyed
faraway
and sent another back, serene,
in his place

to live the day
with the birds
and the light.

CREEDE, 1931

R. E. T. 1884–1948

Fishing the Rio Grande on an August afternoon
after forty years of death and birth—
I *know* you, Grandfather,
with yellow-black grasshoppers clicking in the weeds
and the planet already tilting toward snow:
you have waded mid-river,
backcasting leisurely, a yellow-wash aura
flaring softly from your body, the rocks and trees.
Working up and across, you pop the fly
into the beer-light tails of boulder pools,
where the slate-dull shapes, one after another, rise:
you are not thinking about your family,
not thinking about work, cancer, church,
while placing each felt-soled boot carefully
among the rocks, trying not
to be there, looking up occasionally
as though called, to the bank
where shadow and light move alive
across the granite outcropping with aspen quaking
the river tugging your thighs—dream
on its way to the Gulf, as you reach
the place within range of where he waits,
false casting, taking loops, shooting line
straight from the wrist whipping through the guides
—mending it, allowing the Pale Evening Dun
to fall lightly as a cottonwood seed
onto the jade-smooth run,
bobbing with it, leading over the quiet

hole where you know he'll strike,
exploding through white, his rainbow
silver knife-flashing under the willows,
the hook set with a flick of your wrist
when he breaks into a long, downstream run,
line whining from the reel
you palm for drag, playing him,
one move ahead, going yet staying.
I leave you there in the middle of your life,
in the middle of the river in light.

ORIGINAL SIN AND FORGIVENESS
AT RESTLAND

This is the little monkey face of death:
Thin clown hair; eyes sadly recessed,
Pupils worried as schooling fish,
Then erased bright and vacant—
Accompanied by a flash card smile.

Bones poke the sagging-tent flesh
Drawn in to fetal position:
No more disappearing acts, Grandmother.
Fed on the Black Book and the bile
Of divorced drunk, you forced Mother

To confess "I love you," while whipping her.
I hear the trapped girl in her voice,
"She doesn't know us; she can't understand."
Death-rung, I hold the palsied hand
Shaking the bed. We have a choice.

She doesn't know you; she can't understand.
I remember the fire bells and ice storms of love
Controlled by Mother with a smile—
Dumbfounding heart, then sealing it with fear.
Looking in her black, shiny eyes, I repeat to Grandmother,

Wading impossible quicksand of years,
"I love you."—Perhaps that look had nothing
To do with redemption but hope, that ace we play
To hold on to rags which cover bones.
Mother wavered—*no one is there I know.*

MOONMAN

The indoors-pale, oblong bald head with eyes
We missed; carp-thick lips and Dumbo ears:
Dressed in army surplus khakis all year,
Arms hanging lifeless, he stood on the other side
Of the fence at recess, slack-jawed, gawking, vacant
Behind that nearly puzzled look, arranged
By the stainless steel scalpel of accident.
Our mothers said his body kept growing after his brain
Had stopped, and we could see the fear-struck baby
Inside the unshaved mask of the idiot,
Our own hearts strung with uncertainty,
Wound drawn, cave to cave—mirror and parrot.
Jeering on reflex, we stuck out our tongues
Catcalling, "Moonman, Moonman got no tongue!"
—The world, wolf spider and wolf spider wasp:
His face broke out like chicken pox
When we sprayed him with peashooters. He blinked
And looked at us with Orphan Annie
No-eyes: we laughed and barked inside our dummies
With the flocking black-winged questions razor-beaked.
Alone, he stares at the seesaw tilting
Toward storybook clouds shifting from beast scene
To ballet, and beyond ultraviolet
To Pascal's dread silence inarticulately
Emitting static waves of violence.

RED ANTS

Stung blind as our collie who killed
the rabbits strayed onto our lawn,
Father launched the offensive
each spring, armed with gasoline
and shovel. I was afraid I'd failed

and done something wrong. The ants
trickled along invisible roads
all day between their hill and the field
with loads of seed, cicada wing
and other things they'd stolen or killed

clamped tightly as wedding rings
in their saw-toothed jaws.
"Hold this, boy,"
he'd say, handing me the gasoline;
stomping the steel blade down
into the heart of the ant hill

he'd lift a shovel of dirt and ants,
dump it out, attack again
until the earth ran blurred with ants
swarming, crawling our legs like breath
—locked-in hysteria and death:

larvae hatching seeds of darkness
planted deep, triggering mind tics,
budding blind sight, mouths sickly,
insatiable from the beginning,
incurably strait-jacketed.

He sloshed gasoline over
the silent raging of red ants
then scratched a kitchen match to flame:
we watched them shrivel like cellophane,
hypnotized by the fire and pain,

knowing they'd come again like blight
and he'd raze the world by fire.
Love only stumbled in the way;
nothing I did set it right.
How could I know it was necessary
to be saved?

INDIAHOMA

They have hog-tied it with barbed wire
and hung it headfirst from a fence post;
now rain now sun beyond desire
erase the ligaments from bone.

Mauve-blue impenetrable sky
is lined by an ocean-smooth horizon
of buffalo grass and wild rye.
Nothing moves; and it doesn't occur

to make any sound. Dream-like belief.
What thought its leap for rabbit thought us,
eyeless with frozen grin of teeth—
a meadowlark's flute trills silver,

piercing earth and sky without an echo;
then silence takes hold, and won't let go.

HOW THEY LIVE

One survives from binge to binge,
up on his second charge for manslaughter,
ploughs the fields for his father,
lives in a shack outside of town,
keeps a wildcat for a pet,
and screws a pock-marked Cheyenne—
while the bald one without a hair on his body
drives around the county, viewing his fields and cattle,
pulling teeth on Mondays and Wednesdays,
remaining hooked on Sicily, Patton, TV;
and one takes the high school boys to the motel
for a show of dogs and women on the wall,
whispering as his jockeys bulge;
and one sits on the red bank watching
alternately the evening sun
and white bobber on the breeze-drifted water;
and one rides his bicycle down Main
with a goofy grin and faded baseball cap,
muttering to the butterflies as the raccoon tail
waves in the wind and the cards clothespinned to the spokes
clatter and clatter and clatter;
and one makes the upright attorney's widow,
a dark-haired German immigrant,
forget her sorrow on a white bedspread in the dark
with window raised to the crickets of autumn;
and one stares all day at feet through the green glow
of the foot machine, padding back and forth
from a curtained room, carrying boxes
marked Stetson and Buster Brown, the blotch on his neck
   malignant;

and one drives a cab and burns up in his room
with the wife of the liquor store owner, who sells
all of her gowns and the marriage pictures at an auction
on Sunday; and the one who collects rocks, sells toys and insurance,
decides he's had enough, shuts the door
to the garage and loads the shotgun, never thinking
of those stretches along the Columbia where the agates are perfect;
and the husband and wife team, she an ex-majorette
and he once convicted for stealing hubcaps in Dallas,
eject the blood and bile
in long, clear tubes and inject the embalming fluid,
making everyone look nice, while the one who walks the roads
without a history, without a nose,
puts bottles and cans into a gunny sack,
stops a moment and looks into the crack
between asphalt and dirt, forgetting what it was
as the backdraft of a car tugs her clothes,
a nickel for the sun, a dime for the moon.

RAGGEDY ANN

I was always riding a daydream
Of blurring fields; pins of light
Racing wire like the 'Frisco Zephyr,
While she tramped the county scavenging:
Body rags; face black as lignite;
A chopped off nose—anyone's daughter.

My father, smiling, pointed her out,
"Look, there goes old Raggedy Ann,"
As though she played a curiosity
Straight from Ripley's Believe It or Not:
Gunny sack weighted with bottles and cans,
A scary Santa, haunted empty.

Excited, I would turn and stare,
Hoping to spot the missing nose
As her yellow, bloodshot eyes glanced
From under the red, gypsy-tied scarf,
And she diminished slowly who knows
Down the road into blue distance.

Beyond my simple astonishment,
That look was a bone-reading of sorrow:
She lived the role I acted inside,
Though I couldn't understand what it meant
To break, then choose a silent, narrow
Way, estranged—no place to hide.

For her, the days were dumb as livestock:
Crows, in the backdraft of a car

Floated, resettling to gossip rabbit,
Whose eyes had popped jack-in-the-box—
Each pop bottle was a lucky star,
Redeemed for the two cent deposit.

The furrows flashed like the bright spokes of a wheel,
But against the motionless far horizon
We weren't going anywhere.
Raggedy Ann kept appearing unreal
In a faultless land without crime or passion,
Hearts buried by fear.

CUNNINGHAM BURNS, ELECTRICIAN

Little we know
about Cunningham Burns,
electrician, who was always willing
to light another cigarette, stand,
and jaw awhile, smile, concede
the thickness of the mystery,
who had better things to do
than connect wires in the ceilings
of other men's buildings,
who took to drink and showed up
later and later, who knows why?
Bills, boredom, the football hero son,
the cheerleader daughter, both with
his big nose, but quick,
going places, the vague wife
holding all together
until they scattered like dreams
and he leaked away with cancer,
who spent his life crawling
the rafters in darkness
connecting wires so that men
would have light, commerce,
progress, whose nerves were shot,
spliced with whiskey
which made his jokes spark
and memory short-circuit—
little we know
about Cunningham Burns,
electrician.

CHRISTMAS 1953

Mother stands
with feet correct,
her arm casually
resting on the mantle
the way she's seen
it done in *Ladies'
Home Journal*—
breasts big
under white sweater,
dark lipstick,
smiling at the boys
who sit like Indians
on the braided rug,
stringing popcorn
and cranberries
with needle and thread
beside the big collie
full of leaping,
while Father sits
on the edge of a chair,
hands folded together
on knees, eyes tired,
looking down also at
the boys, but in a daze
as the photographer
says, "O.K., that's it,"
capturing each one
in separate pose,
including the fire

behind glass doors
rushing blurred
from the silent shot
like a spirit
desperate for air.

EASTER 1954

The giant rabbit ate the cookies.
Everyone kneeled, drinking blood from shot glasses.
Over the hill the sky grew black
with thunder and lightning. Women wailed.
A ghost walked among the olive trees talking.
With our Easter baskets full of shredded
cellophane grass, we hunted eggs in city park.
The ducks we never named were purple and orange.
They didn't do anything but squeak
inside their little wire cage with their little bowls
of meal and water. I took a stick
and poked out eyes; the other escaped
into the teeth of the dog.
Father whipped us with his alligator belt.
Mother said it made her sick.
The ducks went to heaven.

THE SUNDAY SCHOOL TEACHER

He wanted Christ because of drink and fear,
And when he said the words his heart felt right.
His children won attendance pins each year
And he took them on hay rides autumn nights.
Unmoved, his shadow waited patiently
For him to think he finally fit in
And the ghosts burning fell like breath in their toy
Bomber through the clear sky—he drank again.
When I last saw him his eyes shone
Serene, but tired of surfacing from Black.
He could see into the wounded child alone
And make him whole with the right word or act.
But why does one believe, another deceive?
He burned to death in bed on Christmas Eve.

CRAWDADS

Down on knees soaked by mud,
With string and a hunk of bacon fat,
We fished for crawdads, wondering at
The lurid depths, hoping a blood-
Sucker bit. Big purplish claws

That'd slice a finger quick as paper.
The slightest tug was met with all
The nerve of catching a hardball—
To draw the thing through murky water
Until it surfaced fat in craw.

BB eyes, black and glinting mean,
Frowned from the helmeted carapace,
While spidery feet waved in space.
We held those ghastly figurines,
Transmitting kindred fear, confusion.

Taken mean, we'd dump the bucket,
Flooding them heaped onto blacktop,
Then watch as they scuttled, stopped, and probed
—The metal shadows rushing above bet
Against their oozing wet intentions.

With each fast crushing snap of life,
I felt the agitated thrill
Of pulling off clothes in a wheatfield,
And cheating at school, telling a lie.
The dark mixed with shadowy light.

Later in July with the creek dry,
I surveyed bones and mud-daubed castles;
The nodding, shaggy sunflowers knew
I had learned not to forgive or cry.
Wasps made a nest of my eyes at night.

"Farmers," he said, "There must have been something wrong
with them." An obese family
whose necks swelled to heads, chewed and talked
with their mouths open—couldn't read or write.

"Horrible," he said, pointing to bits
of glass, scraps of metal twisted like wadded paper,
and in the middle of the road a black patch
where gas and oil exploded.

I heard their animal breathing, mixed with locusts
clicking, the tires rolling on concrete as they pushed—
"They should have had more sense," he scolded.
The glittering stars ripe and long lifeless.

He always told how body was sheared from chassis,
"Like getting hit in the head with a baseball bat,"
and the engine thrown fifty yards from impact.
"It cut a woman in half; can you imagine that?"

In time, rain and sun
washed and bleached away all traces,
so each time we passed I thought, it looks
like nothing ever happened here. But I

had kept the woman-cut-in-half alive,
had saved her from the blank obliterating sun.
With her dwarf's grin, sometimes she performed handstands,
singing while the bottom half tap-danced or soft-shoed,

and sometimes she put herself together again
like my uncle with his funny, sliced-off thumb trick,
anxious to get it right, to please, to bribe
the wasps of guilt, dis-ease, the sorcery

of the fear-blinded, love-confused heart—
"Let that be a lesson to you; don't forget."

MOTHER'S ROSES

On the north side where mint stood high in the charmed shade
Along the wall of leaky faucet, moss and worms—the blade
Of the plains' sun cut curtain-straight two worlds in one:
From that earth dry as a staked hide, and pitiless as vision,
Bloomed Mother's flu-pale roses, their pink tint bled
By the iron oxidized dirt—ancient inland sea bed.
   I filed the hoe to an edge of silver keen enough
To slice my thumb and started chopping, scraping crust
Bone-clean of puncture vine, ragweed and cocklebur,
Whose stony seeds would drift like enemy parachutists over
Our white fence from the wild field and plains next door.
Each smooth, intuitive stroke which severed stem transcended
   chore;
Raked, they looked like a dogpile of green toupees.
    After trenching and damming beds, I'd sit in the house shade
And watch the water lip them, lulled by that bright scene
Of sparrow-chattering trees, dappled shadows of daydream.
But everywhere within the shimmering veneer
The god of terror pricked belief: the mantis praying here,
Mimicking leaf, its cat's eyes frigidly clear, a monarch
Clasped in beak; the eyesockets of the meadowlark
Seething with coffee-grounds-like ants—the dissonance
Fugal, accompanied by Sister's Chopin, strictly cadenced
With Mother's metronome, wills fastened to eternity
Tightly as cicada nymphs—emerging from holes—clamp spiked feet
To branch and molt, backs split for singing metallic beasts.
    Each of us in turn was forced to practice truth and beauty
Bloodless as roses. Children yet, our dream veils
Drawn on Time's sharkgrin; the Wheel's jinxed spin,
We never guessed the merciless lack, thirst deep-rooted in

Her childhood's desert: cowboy Father's flash flood love
Run-off, hardscrabble dry, quick as the rose beds soaked to mud.
Now, another lesson's spleen. Or, is it grace?
Mysterious love guided to perfection, pain embraced?
From her wasting husk a radiant rose unfolds—Faith
Tempered in the blacksun inferno of age.

TEENAGE FUNERAL

We resurrect
the car-struck collie,
the hammer blow
to the hog's head,
the rat-poisoned calico
with anonymous note;
we redream
baby-powdered
grandmothers and grandfathers
with hands folded,
flying nowhere,
the Big Bopper,
Ritchie Valens,
Buddy Holly,
the hired hand
hanged in the silo;
we spin the 45's
of car crash hits:
"Where Oh Where
Can My Baby Be?";
"Dead Man's Curve,"
the love rot sweet
as a bruised peach.

We arrange
and rearrange
your eyes, Egyptian-
shadowed
turquoise blue,
your silly grin,

your spindly legs,
the .38—
lipstick and earrings,
movie magazines,
the puckered Black
drawn tight
as a marble bag,
the faceless man,
radiance
collapsed,
rouged baby cheeks,
glossies of Elvis,
the .38—
your Beatles' bangs,
sneaked cigarettes,
faceless man,
radiance; .38—
nothing fits.

Remorse which can't be cured,
the rest of your life
skips over the scratched
night before,
whiskey leaking
sour as a dishrag
from your pores;
this is the movie
with girl and boxer dog
from the stained Juarez photo;
the gasolined cat
flame-streaking the alley,
the bleeding cottonwood,
maturity in black,

hope dumb as a watermelon
smashed against a windshield
Halloween,
with windows soaped
"Fuck You."

Self-conscious
in Sunday black
and white, too big
or too tight, wool itching,
we don't know
what to do
with hands
before these clouds
of chrysanthemums,
greenery waxed
as Christmas holly:
half irreverently
we pose, assuming
the look of tragedy,
ready to gigglescream,
elbow or slug
the preacher tape-playing
bubble words,
your hands needing touch,
wanting to dig through
flowers, 3-D
against the overcast,
and heal you back
to breath, the sweet
thick body of your
perfume bleeding
to prairie quickly

as the flowers' bouquet
outside their sweating
glass box.

You are the cold
weight of bruise-
colored sky;
you are the crow caw
from the cottonwood
bone white among
branches of smoke
which you are,
and the dry creek
they arch, your church;
you are the switchgrass
gossipping,
the sorrow lodged
like a bullet
in memory,
the vandalized debris
of passion,
blood corsage,
black erasure,
gold leaf tracing
winter plains.

LIGHTNING-STRUCK BOY

Some white folks were living in our negro quarters,
and the old man and boy were chopping cotton—
not in our field, on another man's place,
and the lightning struck and killed
the boy, shot straight down his leg into the ground
and tore off his shoe.
The old man borrowed a car and brought him back.
The sky was violet
with white thunderheads like rapids boiling,
but nothing moved: no bird, no leaf—
like waiting for a pin to drop.
Rigor Mortis had set in, and the old man,
who was short, was bearing upright
the six foot boy tightly wrapped in a sheet
white as chalk against the black and blue
and straight as a string.
His sister came running, crying and telling it
same as a nest-robbed sparrow,
her quick undampered notes
sucked empty by that hot vacuum.
We laid out the corpse on a cot,
I furnished everything nice and clean,
and we bathed the dirt from it:
it looked like he'd been wearing gloves, a mask
and socks of earth; around his head
there was a perfect band of moonlight
where his hat had fit; we washed
until all of him was pale as watered milk,
bathing, paying attention, like prayer—
and then we had one of those tornadoes,

the air swelling like fever, flushing cold to hot
with heat lightning, rain splinters, hail—the freight
roaring, jumping the tracks.
Down in the storm cave
I could hardly think about that poor boy
up there alone, fixed as a vase
with the dull glow reflecting from linoleum,
and that hail drumming the tin roof—
hitting him again.
Next day we buried him in a plain, white pine box,
in a cheap, black cotton suit
paid for by the county, without shoes.
The sister said, "Don't he look nice?
He always wanted to dress right."
I bought a three dollar bunch of flowers
(I knew there'd be none),
and I took the family in the Chrysler.
The county buried him in a pauper's field.
Granite monuments and black-green flames
of cedars marked where the others lay,
but they shared the silence of plains,
that distance which plays tricks on the eyes—
the horizon wavering with heat,
indistinguishable from sky.

TRAINS

When you were a little girl
in Texas, your grandfather
took you to see the trains
come in and leave.
The whole enormous machine
panted, waiting to run,
while strangers got off and on
bound for places Grandfather
would name—Wichita Falls,
Quanah, Estelline,
White Deer, Dalhart.
As the train
pulled away, you waved,
watching it disappear
from the track into a point of sky,
sad in the silence afterward,
holding Grandfather's hand
for the walk home through streets
empty and quiet.
When I was a boy you took me
to see the trains arrive
and depart: I waited near the tracks
to spot the flashing beacon;
the silver engine rippled
on a lake of heat, finally
emerging streamlined,
diesels rumbling the earth;
and the white-jacketed porters
hopped down on the brick ramp
to assist the passengers

who stepped off in their polished shoes,
new suits and dresses, greeting
those who had come to receive them
with smiles, handshakes, hugs—
while others looked on
from the long windows of the chair cars.
We watched them pull away
as they watched us recede,
some waving kindly, indrawn.
I followed the last car
down the inverted V of track
until it became sky.

You took my hand and we walked
away, the world always
distant as we rode home
with nothing to say.
I watched the fields go by,
while you looked down the road
into plains and sky.
                              Today
I notice you look faraway;
the names and dates and places
dissolve into one dream;
you fall asleep in front of the TV;
and I want to say
I didn't understand
the first time,
but if we play it again
I would know what to do—
but distance slowly takes you.

OF AN EVENING

Grandmother would roll the stockings down
around her ankles, sip Coke, and read the news
while I kept us gliding, pushing back on my toes
watching swifts flitter above the town,
cicadas droning in and ebbing from sound.

Grandmother slipped from her body clean
as a cicada, taking dreams of her mother.
Light holds onto the bone-white sycamore;
the lawn is smooth in shadow, velvet green,
neighbors watch TV behind their screen.

A grown-up would float by in a big automobile
absorbed, mysteriously important with purpose—
all streets dead-ended in sky and prairie.
It took me all afternoon, playing tag with girls,
to walk to Grandmother's after school.

Sunset strikes the white frame houses golden;
and grackles yak and splash in the bird bath,
and the toy sidewalks run into grass footpaths.
The old actors have been replaced by children
who, oblivious of their bodies, won't listen.

The neighborhood softens to undersea blue;
a breeze goes out of the trees like a guest from his body.
Sometimes we would sit awhile in the dark and be
silently taken in by the stars, excused
from death—allied with dreams, renewed.

WINTER WHEAT

Many times, as a child,
I stepped into green waves
of a flowing field,
rustling sighs waist deep:

the white-knuckle fist
of fear and lie,
the merciless will
to please

opened, like a morning glory,
all of the stabbing voices
winnowed.

Wind shivered the swells,
flashing silver to dark emerald,
iridescence sweet as the vision of sky
and horizon married
in a yellow dazzle of sun.

Now, after the black hole years,
something persists beyond wish,
with the strength of fields,

beyond reason's bright scalpel
and the futile, slashing knife
of doubt—

something circles back, as I stand in April
on a red road

with my daughters,
before a field of winter wheat,

and walk with them
into the waves and wind.

ALTA

Wind shakes the hedge and bushes,
making a branch tap the window
like a finger.

It's not the dead, the drift of faces
flown from me like leaves in a mad covey
down the street,

but the bright stream of prairie light
through blinds at ten, swirling dust
to warring kingdoms,

floating my bird bones to the edge of skin,
jilting thought light as a feather.
There are times

on the currents of light I'm back in Missouri
with my father the doctor—Mother dead,
her black hair

beautiful in the coffin, Choctaw
cheekbones high and rose-tinted,
rhinestone earrings—

I'm making the rounds with Father in the buggy,
offering gumdrops to the white faces
of diphtheria.

The windows of the neighbor's house
flash bright as mica,
then go black.

I remember that sycamore struck by lightning
in the spring of '43—
a blue blast.

Sometimes I eat chocolates: the ones
with orange centers are best,
my son Milton

brings them from the Five and Dime;
the grocery boy comes at three;
the stray dog

around five, and the Soaps until then,
with cube steak and corn,
the parakeet

whistling tunes. When I crossed the river
into this dry land, I never returned
home again,

grown silent as the dumb chairs in the living room,
a bird-thought among trees of wind—
dust in light.

BALLAD OF A ROAD BOY

This for "Big Ed" Dodson
  who played men's greed for bread,
rode the plains in a Cadillac
  and made it up in his head.

This verse for his sharks, whores, and boxmen,
  the dalmatian-girl act,
the swamp-drowned snitch and the douche bag pimp,
  and for Freddie, who rode out on the Thunderbolt.

And this verse for Big Spring and Odessa
  which float on the heat waves like dreams;
Juarez in the Fifties, good steaks, Theresa,
  a six-dollar room.

This for the hand quicker than
  the eye—dice cup, pool cue,
deck—the slicked back hair, Lewis
  Roth suits; Edwin Clapp shoes.

And for children, white house, picket fence
  —from the outside looking in
a stake beyond the day to day con,
  impossible to win.

The roads which cross the plains are straight;
  they run alone to sky;
so much space and nowhere to go,
  each face the same good-bye.

For twenty years he fought to get sober.
  Finally when he had a year
with apartment, girl friend, job, and car,
  they diagnosed cancer.

No more "cutting up touches" with Sparky,
  Little Virgin, Mainline Slim
or Gene Mann, *catch me if you can*—
  each story dream but him.

The road runs alone to sky.
  One day people glow
like saints, and next punch lines in Death's
  jokes, too dumb to know.

This is for the hard hours
  prayed through, buried by weather,
whining, shaky as a kicked dog—
  the unfisted will a flower.

This verse for the end in a rented room:
  hot plate and TV,
the bullfighter on black velvet,
  clock and Mr. Coffee.

And this for the last phone call, choking
  on blood, the receiver's eerie
voice requesting you dial again,
  hang up and try again.

DEEP RED

Christmas afternoon. The gifts opened
and the wrappers burned; glitter gone
from all but children's eyes, I ride out
into the country with my brother.

Winter wheat glistens keen as fur
across the fields; the cattle are dreams;
the world a postcard mailed from far-
away—so we get out to read.

Armadillos everywhere—
opossum, crow, woodpecker, rabbit.
Hungover from last night, my brother
holds up a turtle shell as though

he'd just won his first merit badge.
After war and divorce, we've come home
to look for bones and feathers in the sand
of a dry river. Cottonwoods stand guard.

I wonder at the blood between us;
how the open world contains
brothers and stars and armadillos—
the strange magnetics of love and hate.

Somewhere ahead, the crows are jabbering.
It's the owl telling them an old story
as light fails deep red
through the black tangle of trees.

II
THE CABIN AT ELK FALLS

ELK AT DUSK

April, the lake has thawed, and there's no cold
To hone silence against the world that shrills
With robins. Driving home on the treadmill
Of rage and dread, which never stop the hole,
You round the curve and find them standing, bold
As only never-fenced beasts could be: still,
In naked meadow bound by aspen hills,
They browse bright discs—pieces of sun—and hold
You there with them, beyond . . . that you might know
Someday daughters who take your hands and lead
You out through boyhood to dream—in fright,
One ear-pricked nerve, they leap into echo
Of hooves knocking deadfall, which silence bleeds
At the trees' bars and forest-filling night.

SIGNS

In the dazzling nothingness of snow
three sets of tracks cross the lake,

their narrowing V intersecting
at scattered bones and frozen hide.

His shadow mocks him
with razor-lined weightlessness.

The gut shot elk must have wandered days
in the dark pines before the coyotes caught

its scent and ran it out onto the ice
where, harassed and fatigued, it slipped

and was ripped to death. This he feels—
the inevitability, like disease,

but he can't read the parallel:
the unnecessary and finally

inexplicable wound which has cut him
from his kind and set him, heart

numb, wandering a labyrinth
through which he's stalked, downwind, by that other

who computes his errors step by step,
and waits for the appointed end.

NIGHT WIND

All night wind poured its river through the pines,
 Lashing the roof and walls,
  Sweeping with obsessive mind
The dream of the body out into winter stars
 Glittering the polished dark.

It sucked at the sills, flaming empty places,
 Dropping in sheering gusts
  Like waves half-crashed to shore,
Down sinkholes of silence under the lost soul's floor
 Where whirl-pool failures, faces,

The whole wound's zero in black wind howling
 Tooth by tooth down the vine
  Of fire from the dead heart
To whatever God it was struck us blind
 From mud and lightning.

PINE AND ASPEN

They stand in foothills facing north:
Bundles of hat pins, flame-shaped cones
With prickle scars, trunks cinnamon-red
To black wrist-thick plates of bark.
The floor is bare of undergrowth,
Combustible, needles and bones;
Spiked branches catch clothes and jab head;
Each step snaps something's back
Brittle as morning-after nerves.
It's hot. The silence stings with horseflies,
True north impossible with will
Haywire as a compass metal-locked,
Tree after tree compounding blur;
For company, the bickering cries
Of squirrel or jay's nest-robbing squawk—
No comfort, nor any promise of it.

* * *

White grove green-shimmering, facing south
In a cleft at valley's end, muledeer woods:
Smooth trunks protrude black
Egyptian eyes, unmoving mirrored quiet;
Soft undergrowth
Is dotted yellow, red,
Blue and lilac
With paintbrush, columbine, wild iris.
The shade is soothing to the nerves.
The dazzling silver-green quaking of leaves chinked
With light sounds like a stream;

Here is a spring surrounded by damp moss
And shooting stars—
Now try to hold this dream
Without thinking,
Without remembering what's lost.

DAYBREAK ON THE NORTH FORK

Dog and I shipped into the dark with our heads
facing east, and now we wake

from nightmare or rest in that cold dark before
dawn with bird cries, with ridge light

breaking from ultramarine blue to ash, with
the camp still in chill shade and

skimmed with dew: letting the hands make the way, I
snap twigs and build a tepee,

scratch a safety match to the blessing of first
flame, wait for the kindling with

the same quiet warmth as from a run of luck,
place branch on igniting branch

until it pops cinders, consuming itself
like joy, waves rippling air

like a mirage, with the scorched black coffee pot
already perking, and light

new and clear on the meadow where butterflies
are busy working yellow

by the stream's silver scaled snake sidewinding green
—for once, I'm nowhere but here.

THE CABIN AT ELK FALLS

"Dark is a way and light is a place . . . ."
DYLAN THOMAS

After the war Doc Tynan moved in,
Trying to treat the dead men's eyes
With aspen and gold sunrise,
But what they needed was more morphine;

Fixed, he'd sit and watch the woodpile
Burn amber and dusk fall adagio,
Or snow filling the cold meadow
Until he healed them all in April.

Then Price, half gone with cancer, came
With his wife: wheeled by rounds of despair
And hope, they made little repairs,
Kept the fire stoked, and thought it home.

Wild strawberries gathered in August,
Water daily drawn from the spring,
Feeding the birds, woodcutting, cooking—
Through certain dark, enough to trust.

I didn't come here looking for peace,
But escape from failure, God and lie,
Carrying a loaded gun inside,
Doctoring the black hole with whiskey.

I received dead tree, dead stone, dead bird,
Dead sky, dead sun, dead prayer, dead stream
And believed—even as in a dream
The road became a burning door.

WHITEOUT

I sit and watch the storm come in
Late afternoon. The far blue range
Has disappeared, and now the ridge
Across the valley too is gone.

Sound waves soften past breathing.
The contours of the hill above
The meadow float through gauzy white.
Pines wash into dark shapes alone.

Out of his usual daylight concealment,
A coyote trots across the clearing:
How easily he moves, at one
With silence, whiteness—invisible

To predator and prey alike,
Before and after never fought.
Soon the phone lines will be down
And the road blown and drifted deep.

I have my friends the fire and whiskey.
This growing blindness that I crave
Seems merciful, almost a cure
This burial in snow and wind.

The coyote's snowshoe circles when
Pursued like a man lost—I could not
See the hellfire heart was love,
That no way in means no way out.

SPLITTING WOOD

I heft the sledge above my head
and swing it down squarely against
the wedge ringing, log bucking apart
clean and white as a sliced apple,
sun-flesh no man has seen.

No analysis today: I toss
the knotted ones into a pile
where they can lie until I'm cold;
I know the way of will,
how wedges bury and axe binds

in twisted grain, against whorled spikes
of branches hard as hate,
the pain stored in that dumb matter
a lifetime's secret bludgeoning guilt,
daggers of *if*. Today I'm after

the tone of honest work, heart song,
the sapling core from which all rings
ripple to light full-flamed
as the aspen leaves' yellow desire,
a drowsy rasping in smoky weeds.

Sun and work burn into shoulders,
sweating armpits and crotch
(the slabs will stack snug as quatrains):
each unflinching stroke flows
from eye to hand fusing muscles

and bones to a wave outrunning thought,
seams riven from inside
exploding a bouquet of resin,
momentum's edge holding the beat
like a wheel spinning standing still.

GREAT HORNED OWL

Across the lake, in lake-still twilight,
I halfway sense a shape not rock
Shift the contour of the black outcrop.
Thought quickly displacing fright

Can't hold in ultramarine blue
Shading to indigo, to dream
In which a shape from stone takes wing
Silently, spirit thrusting through

The years' blinded, deadweight life
In a burning, gold-eyed rush of awe,
Until I cleave to terror and fall—
A demon bird swooping through sky

At my back, talons cocked, shadow
Accusing "Whoo—Whoo," snapping beak
As I run between black walls of trees,
Turning to stone down the nightroad.

COYOTE NIGHTS

Sleepless, cut off
in dead sea dark,
no word to say it . . .
from granite bedrock
and pines a howl
rushes the spine
like a brush fire,
flashes up from
the gut, hackling
neck hair, from cave
climbs the ladder
through blood hunting:
brother in wound,
from head thrown back
to heaven, piercing,
it rises, lungs
bursting with night,
breath blown
through the throat hole
resonating
bone, rising;
tongue speechless, flat
against the roof,
clearing teeth,
lip-shaped zero
burning like rabies
it rises, thrust
to stars' glinting
knives—where it seems
to hold, an instant

of endless ripples
in after-howl,
before the maw
of incurable silence—
and you, gifted
with desperation,
must start again,
needing more dark,
more ballast-hope
jettisoned for song.

LIGHTNING-STRUCK PINE

"Some of them will stay almost well always."
LOUISE BOGAN

Sometimes I notice one
stands out among the others,
a yellow gash black-bordered
slicing the length of trunk.

The other half is green
with needle boughs waving
in a slight breeze; but most don't
scar right—weakened by the blast

they cripple on a few
seasons, then the fire beetles
scout a way in and burrow
to heartwood for the coup.

Though this one appears to grow
as others, buried the blow that
burnt to roots like someone
diseased recovered from

the hopelessness that kills,
it's more a cold rage kept
stoked by some regret, some-
thing unforgiven no will

could cure: long after green
has fallen to forest floor in
decay's slow burning—
this resin-fist ready
   for flame.

RUN-OFF

Between the red-tailed hawks'
April daredevil air show mating
and the June meadow's riot
of dandelion sun money for elks,
all day and all night for days
snowmelt and thawing earth
plunge water down the gully,
caving the banks and tumbling
deadfall—like mysterious
love blasting a way
through the fear-dammed heart,
it jumps the creek, steering
sun-flashed quicksilver rivulets
through aspen, racing unseen paths
like grace, setting some tuning fork
of blood and bone humming,
until the body is an ear
ringing, immersed in the glory of going
chiming elsewhere: it fans out
across the meadow grass, like tide
sweeping seaweed
under a rippling sheet of glass,
driving up earthworms for robins and kinglets,
dropping down hill out of sight;
one day it's gone—leaving silence
struck by a deeper silence
holding you for days
like the blazing shadow of lost love,
even after all running paths

are a chaos of dry stones,
and the creek within its bed
meanders sparkling through the meadow,
slowing toward the trickling shallows of autumn
and first ice.

SANGRE DE CRISTO, JULY 4

Lightning strikes talus, rips
breath-quick, clapping dryly off cliffs
steel-thick, and rumbles down
the valley out of sound.

Fat, syncopated drops now
hop from dust and spatter bough,
ricochet off tent and skillet,
hit the lake like cold bullets

of hail, crescendoing
to silk-thin sheets gusting
ghostlike, its taut surface drummed
to effervescence—

soothing, releasing daydream
from fear as the Svea hisses steaming
rice, our tin cups ready; gifts
like rain and the risk

of love which brought us to these rocks
and sky. This spread-eagle peak, whose cirque
returns our voices to nothing,
was uplifted from molten

waves fused like passion heart-deep,
compressed feldspar and quartz
glassy as the light shimmering in
your eyes, whose cavedark I enter,

afraid as the man inside my dream
of collapsing floor and endless falling.
Waking is slow as a flower
opening—crisp-scented weather

of the wet meadow grass; and clouds
burning off the granite-proud
eagle, its perfectly clear shape
reflected on the breathless lake—

then, a splash—and another splash,
until the wings are shattered glass
and the whole surface ringing pools
of silver-flamed cutthroats leaping.

HOW THE DEAD COME BACK

for Walter Hall

"But even something as solid as hair slicked down by epoxy on a lead
golfball is as elusive beyond superficial touch as what it is like to be
somebody else and how to talk to them that they'll know you did and join
you vibrating through nightlight prisms of luna moth's wings."
WALTER HALL, *Miners Getting Off the Graveyard*

Sometimes, when I'm driving in my blue truck alone,
you quietly slide into the blank space
of the passenger's side, and we're four-wheeling at dawn
up a wagon road, middle of the San Juans,
heading to a high meadow for elk: gears moan
as we crawl over chuckholes and rocks in low,
droning the only sound in the cold silence
of overcast, against the mountain's bare
aspens like smoke among dark evergreens,
snow now dusting the road—I wish I'd stayed
home, but you joke me back to wheel and rocks,
cackling with the same devilish grin you made
on introducing me to friends: "This summer
he came to read his poetry, and now
he's returned to kill." Perhaps that's why you come back
in the blank space at empty times, to remind
me it's all wilderness, to hone the edge.
You appear, as though by touching a fetich's heart,
in your blue bathrobe, slippers and Stetson at dawn,
laughing white teeth and ice-blue berserker's eyes,

firing a .44 wake-up call,
cracking off canyon walls above the roar
of Willow Creek, wind rocking pines and aspens
3-D as your elk chile and wild raspberry pie:
that ramshackle miner's cabin you camped in,
built into the cliff. "A boulder might
come crashing through your bedroom anytime,"
you'd say with relish, telling a guest good-night—
the crushing gravity of that mountain life
you mined like the pure silver buried in veins
of amethyst, compassion's lode from loss,
a crazy faith in balancing the heights;
though I can't remember what we talked about
those mornings at the kitchen table over
coffee, we talked across the place where all
props fail and memories are rained away
like earth; though you repeated you were a fart
like the rest of us down here, jealous with lust,
petty from pride, we must have talked the fist
into a flower, recalled how, above
the cliff, it levels to plateau at ten thousand,
and you can easily walk on sun
after sun, where they scattered your ashes July.

III
EVIL AND FLOWER

EVIL AND FLOWER

for Eryn

The ice pick ear ache at three;
Fevers from cutting teeth,
Attack and disappear
Suddenly as night fear
Of thunder, wind, lightning
Opens on a spring morning
Washed clean by rain and light.

Drunk with the tree-bloomed sky
You name the leaves Flower—
Birds vanishing in air;
Your stumbling tip toe run
Is flight—I warn,
But watch you go alone,
Joy outdistancing bone.

WITH CAITLIN AFTER RAIN

Caged by gray inside—
Hard bread of weak faith,
My heart numb as a face
Shot with novocaine—
You shout and beg me outside

To view the day's remains:
Clipped, synthetic greens
With sidewalks washed stage-clean,
Tedium of robins—
Everything explained.

You chase a cat and splash in
Puddles; your sky blooms
Airplane and moon:
I try recapturing
    the glow,
But the door back is hidden;

So I explain shadows
And understand, a mime.
You take my hand and climb
Onto a ledge, guiding
Where I need to go:

The wind through leaves in light
After rain says how we live:
You lead me to the rose;
I teach you quartz and granite.
We name the mourning dove.

THIS MORNING YOU WILL WAKE

This morning you will wake and look
into the mirror at the face
freshened by sleep.

You will begin applying makeup;
brushing the hair to what shape
you think adequately beautiful,

and then you will dress and walk
to work, in an absence of birds,
in an abundance of bare branches.

Your spirit rises to the edge
of flesh to embrace cold air,
the lawns raked, still green.

You will remember the deep blue
thunderstorms of summer widening
with sheet lightning over plateaus,

the river full of bright water
on bright mornings full of birds;
roads which roll and straighten

to nowhere in the plenty of time:
an ordinary song to sing amidst
an extraordinary recurring dream.

MISCARRIAGE

The day before, a freak blast of hail
stripped the leaves like locusts,
fashioning a garden of black juices and spikes,
pitting the melons, cracking their vines
to dried umbilical cords, knocking tomatoes green
to the ground, neatly shedding a dead dress of leaves
around the base of each tree.

Last night the cold moved in with a full moon
and blood. (Some thing knew something.)
Your body contracted like a drunk's
with the dry heaves, laboring with death—
hope and fear adrift
in the middle-of-the-ocean dark.

I rake the leaves; I rake
as our daughter wanders circles under a sky
washed bruise; I rake as the painkiller drops you to sleep.
The gray-green undersides of maple leaves
are scattered like fish belly up in a lake,
their black fingers curled back brittle;
I rake them into piles the wind takes;
I rake as blackbirds of hot light
and stainless steel with blood bright as spray paint
strafe and peck the nerves to bits.
I rake into the night.

—Now the movie of glass children, each word
an incision. What you have seen you haven't seen,
but know by the hole it makes in you

through which all of the whys fall,
trapped like crazy sparrows that continue
building the nest after the chicken hawk.

In your nightmare you try fitting its head back
onto its body, grasping it slippery as a trout.
I drive to work outside my body;
you slice tomatoes full of blood.
One evening, we share the only melon
ripe enough to harvest from the hail,
while our daughter, her red hair glistening,
dances to wind and light.

BIRTH

for my wife and daughters

And we set in with sun
    at the spring-jeweled headwaters
Brimming the banks
    bright with April,
Bees in the blood
    whirling for blooms.
We floated far
    from the familiar
When the rumble of rapids
    roiled distance,
Too late to lay
    for lee of shore—
I watched the whirlpool
    suck us winding
Bound to bottom
    breathless,
And prayed to move with the muscle
    of current moiling,
Drawing through dark
    voluminous dare,
With each stroke the screw
    in spine driven,
Your face sunflowering
    fire heart-full:

We backswept to brake
                    around a bend,
But slammed the stern
                    squealing against
Cliff—the cord
                cut, twisted
From neck like a noose,
                        we knifed through narrows
Into the channel coaching
                        over roar to clear
Boulders, deep-breathing,
                        pushing, rebounding
Wave-shocked, bow straight
                        into white squall,
Time shed with spray
                    like sparks, when we're dropped
Running rips
            through the chute with roof
Blown to blue
            breath-held sky:
Then the bald bruised
                    bloody holy cry,
And we wake,
            baptised in the waves'
Sloshing haystacks
                on slackwater
Winedark, drifting
                drawn toward the Gulf,
The shore slowly
                refocusing in sun,
Lemon-lime
            tinted leaves,
City cars
        concrete rush hour,

The people dull puzzles
                    locked apart
About their business
                    backlit, dressed
In light alone,
           guests longing like us
In the fierce flow
           forward, blessed.

VISIONS OF A BONE HUNTER

Loren Eiseley, 1905–1978

After the deaf mad mother and T.B.,
Depression years of riding rails across
Desert, and father transposed to dreams and dust—
You wake, guided to childhood reverie,

Uncovering the gift for bones intact.
Begin in the Badlands on knees, disguised
As a Ph.D., a shaman seeking Light
For something whole, direction to take back

For the tribe—exhuming mineralized teeth,
A femur brown as oakwood, piece of skull
Protruding from the ash-gray gully wall,
Extinction like hard rain cutting belief:

Titanotheres, herds of terrier-sized
Dawn horses, dirk-toothed cat and the dire wolf . . .
Until, like them, you're carbon traced in cliff,
Powerless, nothing known to theorize

At twilight, looking on moon-desolate
Ravines, labyrinthine as cerebrum:
Silence not bound to kindness; vacuum
Which stabs the heart Black—locked in grief's deadweight.

Far, as in dream, you hear, then see, the birds
Contracting, expanding thumbprint, carbon snaking
Its rope of fire over the darkness, singing . . .
This way, it says, fading on the north wind.

Some nights there is no sign; insomniac,
Outwait what waits below, terror of shape
Shifting in blood and bone: the snout agape
For air, stuck through Devonian mud flat;

Scales shed, the backbone arch lifts belly free
From earth, though the tail drags; the heart divides:
Cold-blooded perfect claws, slit yellow eyes;
The nose-brain bunches hemispheres to see

The nervous night and scent, to aim the head . . .
Twittering, a cockroach crunched in ratlike teeth.
The crack you see in all God's made rots faith.
On desk and office wall you touch the dead

Things' medicine—an ice-age bison skull,
Indecipherable alphabet cone
Not chance, and past utility, a stone
Hand-ax smoothed for the feel, made beautiful—

Until the mystery of flowers and fire
Heals you from doubt to carrier of ladders
At the Black's edge, become a star thrower.
But, tired, you hear the whirlwind's voice . . .

MOTHER WAITING

The background blurs from sleep to sleep,
with pills at nine and morning toast.
He bathes and dresses me; he cuts
the meat and bits of fruit; I add
some rouge before the mirror,
my gray hair wild as a baby's.

On this side, doctor visits and family:
they repeat the same non-answer,
"We will just have to wait and see."
Upstarts, knowing nothing, feeling nothing,
can't remedy the burning tongue
or restore a crumbling memory.

The children phone long distance,
sensing the floor giving way;
I transpose their names; they
happened long ago; my grand-
daughter babbles like me, she takes
each step breathlessly.

In this limbo the movie
changes: my husband is the clever
stranger impersonating my husband,
doctoring my food, selling the house
behind my back; as he watches TV
crime stories, I sit against a wall

wrapped in a blanket of silence,
rotting from the head down, one eye

wandering while the other fixes on nowhere
or haunts the past, where my people wait—
and God everyday. Pain

says the prayers, the dull
nausea which grinds me down
to a whimpering thing, then terrorizes
suddenly—a door flung open,
wind scattering the props,
the new script full of masks.

What lesson I must learn from this
on top of age, I do not know;
and now they are here, their caroling faces
lit by the flickering lights
on the white-iced cake, and dressed in my new

blue gown, wishing, I step across
and blow out the candles.

PAIN FUGUE

I wake in the middle of night with enchiladas
twisting intestines tight as fence wire, gas corrosive,
the mysteriously inflamed jaw throbbing skull,
reminding I've forgotten to insert the mouthpiece
which prevents teeth cracking, chipping, grinding
to nubs from what else but *waking?*—out-on-a-limb rat-racing,
when the gimp tendon kicks in, torn practicing
karate punches that force King Sloth to distance,
and I hear my pregnant wife wandering the house,
tortured to life by the 7 lb. vampire leeching calcium
from her bones, pinching nerves, kicking bladder;
she's rummaging the fridge for pickles and sherbert—
Listen! the five-year-old's up groaning,
cotton-mouthed, sweating orphans and tornadoes;
I glance at the two-year-old conked out in ballet slippers,
recall how she whipped us all weekend with the "No, No, No's,"
the golden curled, fascist fairy slashing her kingdom from jungle;
she'd have us duct-taped and car-trunked in a blink
since it burns, coming up or going down,
though we keep thumb sucking and babbling tales each way;
any wonder our eyes are dilated as TV zombies',
our brains shocked specimens of a lifelong experiment—
the amplified voice of Father booms from the hinterland
"You're spoiling those kids rotten," corroborating my Swiss cheese
conscience, but the wife's quit feeding and wandering after strokes
and clichés of solace, though insufficient for sleep,
and I'm snuggling the five-year-old into oblivion

(pray the two-year-old doesn't telepathically detect missed chaos):
this one's little white arms, freckles, Viking princess's red hair,
how we're forced to love and miracle through pain,
compassion solid as the healing belonging sung in the old hymns,
though it never holds the tide of hard labor, nightmare, decay.

CLOSING TIME AT THE ZOO

The crowd, like smoke, a dream
with laughter and scream
and that low warming hum of the species,
has disappeared—balloons, ice cream,
beer and dolls, flowed through the gate
in sunglasses and tired smiles
in the late winter sun; rays flash

the mallards' dark necks metallic,
spark eyes to rubies
and dust mottled breasts amber,
back-light my wife and daughter like angels,
gold leaf the black tangle
of branches from which mountains rise,
burning an aura of lake-rippled light.

perched rock-solid among boulders,
bald pate and Roman beak tucked neatly
between shoulders, eyes watching,
zooming in what moves beyond the wire,

vigilant as the beast sensing dis-ease,
wound-never-healed, probing for
an opening—pride, envy, fear—
conjuring, whispering, pecking

—Our daughter toddling wino-tipsy
babbles praise for the peacock's display, mocking
my drama with her magic play . . .

I join the cacophony of meowing,
refusing heart-close doom out-of-nowhere,
embracing blood and breath, moved by light
within, though I feel the wolf
fix on her wild, joyous shape
from its fenced lair of pines and packed earth,
clench her between jaws a last long second
after we've disappeared into night, into the world.

FAT PEOPLE AT THE AMUSEMENT PARK

They are laughing like the rest of us,
amused at being here
among bright lights and whirling things

laughing, despite their particular knowledge
of gravity, which is why they ride
the fastest and highest rides,

a release from the demands of earth
between bouts with blue cotton candy,
stuffed bears and peanuts—

we watch them bounce along the midway
with their rosy-cheeked smiles and jouncing
asses, chattering as though they'd entered

the kingdom, they step into the cars
of the tilt-a-whirl, tilting, and take off
into a scream of weightlessness.

A GOOD NIGHT'S SLEEP

And now I see the black and white cows
grazing on the long green
which slopes up the cliffs to blue.

Inland, the clocks tick each digit away
silent as feathers being buried in snow.

Fathers are putting on their clothes,
walking backwards out of other men's bedrooms

as the suicide staring into the river
begins singing, and the teenagers wild

with booze decide not to crash through
the brick wall which floats into the air,

and the physicists nostalgically dismantle
the symmetry of holocaust—it is Christmas

Halloween Valentine's Day Easter New Years
when Mother's arms open, her hands

the long watering animals of dreamland.
I see the black and white cows

flying away into the blue, their wings amber,
flying low over the water, silently out
into the green horizon of the Pacific.

MR. NORWOOD

He stands at the foot of my bed
expressionless and mute,
inside a white room, walls
vague as drifting snow,
waiting with his long-suffering wife,
her Buddha smile, as though
I should have expected them.

In drunken oblivion he missed a curve
years ago, was paralyzed forever
before he died.

I visited to play Daniel Boone
with his son; we walked through the room
where he was propped in bed
on white pillows, head faced toward the wall
open eyed, not looking—
like a thought lost.

Perhaps he is summoned by the suffering
which wakes me to the dark, ocean-night
alone beside my sleeping wife.

There are others like him
who come to share
distance, hearts softened,

who sense the residue of grief,
black rose.

And I never send them away,
and they never know what
to say.

LOST

The same houses stand
The people die and
Others move in, tell
Their stories and dis-
Appear; the meadow
Fills with trees, bleached bones;
The town on the plain
Succumbs to grass and
Wind; wind and ice
Erase the mountains;
Everywhere I
Look there is no place
To begin from, our
Faces change into
Our mothers' and our
Fathers', into those
We have never known;
On walks leaves shadow
Puzzles across walls
Then all is darkness,
Silence when we wake
Exhausted from some
Place we can't recall,
While time devours
Like ants dismantling
A prize butterfly,
And in age our mates
Turn strangers and die
Saying they never
Knew us, our bodies

Worked into juice by
Bacteria and
Grubs, the bones at last
Carbon reclaimed by
Dirt, with our names snowed
From the fallen stones—
Where we begin each
Day, shoved out the door
By the pikes of fear,
Blessed pain which moves
Us desperadoes
To faith through the wilds
Of air, our paths
Closing behind us
Traceless as the wakes
Of little sailboats
In a giant race.

BREAKDOWN

It weaves the plot out near the edge
Like a hurricane at sea
While moving inland gradually;
The people look and talk

With no one inside; they pull apart
Like dolls with little arms,
Whispering how they'll harm
You once they find a way inside;

You grip the steering wheel with hands
That look like yours; you speak
And dress and brush your teeth,
But you know—its hydraulics

Are locked on full capacity
When it strikes, lashing out
With gale-force rage and blackout—
Miracuously you wake in the eye,

And then it snaps—power like that
Doesn't let go—and what you thought
Made it work is lost.
The place you never own is restored:

See how the patient hands work
The pieces with the mind;
Though you can hear at times
Like these some shape snarling trapped

In undergrowth deep in the forest.
See how a life renews
Itself quietly, continues
Unremarkably each day,

The heart beginning to listen, the hands
Obedient to reprieve;
Every moment you breathe,
Everything you do is prayer.

FOR JAMES RILEY

"And therefore be now content to consider with me, how to this
'God the Lord belong the issues of Death' (Ps 68:20)."
JOHN DONNE, *Deaths Duell*

Efficient tax accountant that you were,
You've closed receivable and payable,
Disconnected computer terminals.

All autumn we have driven past the park
To treatment—seen the beds of zinnia fire,
And in the blue coolness of recessed firs

The graceful players dressed in summer white,
And girls on the bike path jogging in flimsy
Shorts we joke about, recalling the Sixties

We drank away. After radium,
You nod in sun as we hit the chromium
Glare and glass glint of the Interstate.

That was months ago: the flower beds are ploughed
Mounds and the mica leaves of the cottonwood
Fallen and scattered where the players stood.

Remission failed with hope, like gossamer
Shot out on calm, ballooning, grounds if air
Cools imperceptibly. Slumped in a wheelchair,

You wait with me in the hospital lobby
For John to bring the car, unshaven face
Jaundiced and sunk to skull—bodies racing

Like flies around us—life erased to blur,
In which I am whomever you accuse,
Eyes glazed and angry from morphine and truth.

In silence, metastasizing cells continue
Swelling the black tumorous veins to claws.
We throw fire-prayers into the maw.

At dark we drive you home through the rush hour
Of rain-streaked, fever-petaled Christmas lights,
Disintegrating blooms on a glass night—

And carry you up the stairs and set you down
In front of the TV, where aliens
Try explaining from where and why they've come.

The room clears; we forgive the wounds
Unhealed; and naked by grace kiss good-bye—
Your eyes' deathless, blood-flowering rush of light.

LETTER IN MIDDLE AGE TO MY EX-WIFE,
NOT MAILED

The apartment building we survived was leveled
To field, for sale the last several years:
Each time I pass I note the concrete steps
Leading nowhere, the tree I stood below
At the corner bare in snow, then full of leaves
And birds, the sidewalk where we came and went.
They've strung a tall wire fence around it all
As though someone could deface dirt, with a sign
KEEP OUT (this emptiness is mine alone).
Sometimes I find your garret of light and plants
On the third floor of air, the place of solace
You lacked, or the thin reclusive sisters downstairs,
Quiet as I became, frightened by our fights;
I'm always dead in an overcoat at the curb,
Waiting for the light, headed to the Avenue Bar
To bury myself till day or binge with "friends"—
Vets, pensioners and whores laughing in the cave,
Telling one story, smelling of flat beer:
Now, face-lifted, behind immaculately
Squeegeed windows dine tables of pinstriped yuppies
Whose pagers beep strategic business dates,
Who walk straight lines and do not drown in dreams.
Two weeks ago in early morning dark
With streets deserted, I drove home alone
After the birth of my son—the one you wanted—
The Christmas-lighted bar and black hole lot
Made a strange scene I had and had not played;
Tired, disbelief mixed with the glow of blessing,
Floating on the planet light as a toy boat

Over a bottomless lake, I looked across
At another man alone inside his car,
And stared at the neck stalk supporting head
Held still, focused on the dark street in front
Of us, wondering where he came from, where
He was bound so late, humbled by how . . . forgiveness,
While waiting there in silence for the light.

ABOUT THE AUTHOR

Rawdon Tomlinson grew up in the farm and ranch country of southwestern Oklahoma. He has taught literature and writing at Metropolitan State College and at the University of Denver, where he received his Ph.D. His poems have been published widely in many journals, in the chapbook *Down Under It All* (1971), and in the collection *Touching the Dead* (1979). He lives with his wife and three daughters in Denver, Colorado.

Photo by Tom Ebey